# The Path of
# Least Resistance

Eric Coleman

The Empath of Least Resistance © 2023
Eric Coleman

All rights reserved.

Presentation by *BookLeaf Publishing*

Web: www.bookleafpub.com

E-mail: info@bookleafpub.com

ISBN: 9789357212557

First edition 2023

*To my daughters, Amelia and Elizabeth, for being the inspiration to keep going- You are my sunshine, and Daddy loves you both.*

*To my best friend Rusty, for pushing me to write and being my sounding board.*

# PREFACE

The first trio of poems were from my high school years, as I experienced my first love. Moving on from there, it becomes more complex and less happy, while I struggle with various life obstacles including depression and divorce. Finally, some poems of self discovery and acceptance, as things start to look up.

# Someday

Someday my love,
You will understand,
The depths of my affection.
Til that day,
I will attempt,
To show without misdirection.
You are valuable
Dear to me,
But not a possession.
Frankly, I'll admit
That you've become
Simply put, a slight obsession.

Someday my love,
You and I
Will join as one and marry.
I cannot wait
For that day
When we no longer tarry.
But instead leave
Our old life,
Courageous together, no longer wary
No matter what
I'll love you
And your cross I'll carry.

Someday my love,
We will fade
Lose our lives, or go insane.
People will forget
(Oft they do)
When we are final lain
Before we pass
We can remember
Our life together, very fain.
But always know,
When I die,
My love will still remain.

# Soon

Soon, my love
Our fight will
Cease, and we'll have won.
We can't be
Kept apart for
Long, our separation nigh done.
I dare them,
To extend torture
And prevent happiness of their son.
I gladly choose
You o'er them,
I mind not, if away we must run.

Soon, my love
Our fight will
Matter not, if ye die.
I ask you,
No, I beg,
To seek aid and not lie.
The unknown frightens,
Scares me so,
For I know not what'll become of you and I.
I feel hopeless,
Watching you hurt,
My love in part the reason why.

Soon, my love
I'll take care
Of you myself, no doubt.
If you grow old,
Weak and tired,
For you I'll remain strong and stout.
I'll be here
Always for you,
No more reasons for you to pout.
I worry so,
For many reasons,
But mainly your love, I can't live without.

# My Love

My love, mine
Lady so fair
How'd I manage to woo?
Three long years
Of constant effort
Helped me to win you.
But right now,
Times are tough
And I don't know what to do.
So help me
Give me direction
Because I'm lost too.

My love, mine
Never doubt me
For my love is strong
Stand by me
Forgive me please
Ne'er again will I do you wrong.
Please just wait
Patiently, that's key
And remember that it won't be long.
Til I leave
The tyrant's grasp,
And we can write our love song.

My love, mine
I beseech you
To listen to my plea.
Stay strong always
Don't fret so
And just wait to see.
My affection and
My devotion will
Last, and never cease to be.
I love you
Forever and always
Someday soon my love, you will marry me.

# It's Cold

It's cold.
The biting wind
and nipping snow,
bitterly assault my cheeks,
hiding the presence of tears
that have lived here for weeks.

It's cold.
The hard concrete
and sturdy oak,
stand stoic to show,
reminding where you lay at rest,
or at least where a body should go.

It's cold.
I'm lonely at your grave,
and sadly it's true,
that they came along that drive
and left this world with you.

It's cold.
In my hands is a box,
containing the essence of three.
Ashes of my true loves,
now gone forever from me.

It's cold.
I have come here today,
to remember, as in years past
like every year, when the first snow falls
and the pain returns, fresh and vast.

It's cold.
I should have been by your side,
But I stayed alone.
The girls rode along, so I longed,
to hear you on the phone.

It's cold.
Same as it was the night,
that damn driver drank.
And I listened to you scream,
when he hit you like a tank.

It's cold.
I shouted for you, all three.
As sirens screamed, drowning out
my voice, going hoarse
Raw and ignored along the interstate route.

It's cold.
And I was numb, when they arrived
Crying on the porch that you asked me
for but will never walk on again,

Except in my memory.

It's cold.
I'm leaning by the tree
ashes spread all around.
On my face, in my hands, scattered
Like my mind, no longer sound.

It's cold.
I have tried to fix my broken heart
To move on from my pain
But I ache even after all this time,
And so by your side, I've lain.

It's cold.
The only way to escape this hell
Is to leave it behind, this act a crime.
And as I drift off for final sleep,
I smile because I feel one last time.

I feel cold.

# Little Firefly

Oh little Firefly,
Why do you cry?
Who clipped your wings,
So you can't fly?

Oh little Firefly,
Why are you sad?
Who crushed your spark,
And all the dreams you had?

Oh little Firefly,
Why aren't you mad?
At those who hurt you,
And treated you bad?

Oh little Firefly,
Show yourself some grace.
Don't blame yourself,
Or think to hide your face.

Oh little Firefly,
Try and smile once more.
It's a beautiful thing to see,
That which I long for.

Oh little Firefly,
Go forth and shine!
I want to help you rise,
And one day call you mine.

Oh little Firefly,
So brave and tough.
Remember all the wonderful things you are,
And especially, that you are enough.

# Again

Again.
What a versatile word.
Scary, mostly.
But there are some
Positive takes.
Like, trying
Again.
Succeeding
Again.

But why am I afraid?
Because! Imagine
Getting hurt
Again.
Falling apart
Again.
Failing miserably
Again.

Why would I try
Again?
Why SHOULD I,
When giving up
Is easier and safer,
Than losing everything
Again?

What scares me? You ask
Again.
More than never leaving
What I needed to escape,
Is the knowledge
That I would do it all
Again.

# Unlove

"Love's a fickle thing
Fallen from old grace.
Once esteemed by ring
A laughingstock now
To the human race.

There is no love though
True chivalry dead.
At least I thought so,
Til we met and
You got in my head.

I'm told this is wrong
To pledge myself pure.
But when you feel strong
For one gal alone,
They got the wrong cure.

Heart and mind agree
Ain't much I can do.
But what you can see
Though I try and run,
I can't unlove you."

Ah, how time flies
Though the days seemed long.
A prisoner unaware of his sentence,
Thought himself shackled by love,
But oh, how he was wrong.

These words above
I wrote in naivety.
From a time now gone
Of my commitment to you,
While you started to unlove me.

# Too Long

It's been too long
SInce we last talked
And my mind begins to wander.

Much too long
Since we last walked
And makes me start to ponder.

It's been too long
Since I've shown you,
The face behind the mask.

Much too long
Since my smile too
Felt unlike a task.

It's been too long
Since I've loved you
The way you want, you know.

Much too long,
Since I've shown you
I don't want you to go.

# My Sun Shine

There was a storm the day we met,
Time stood still and thunder cheered.
Announcing your arrival,
My eldest daughter appeared.

I had no idea then,
How much you would change me.
How deep I could love,
Or how worried I could be.

I knew I wasn't ready for fatherhood,
(Many very seldom are)
But I guess you were ready for me,
So how could I deny you, my little star?

I do not regret,
The sleep I've gone without.
And every little laugh,
Is worth every single pout.

I only hope that I can teach,
What I was never taught.
Love and patience unconditional,
So you are never fraught.

My desire for you,
To be better than I,
But still choose to keep,
My memory alive.

Every day you grow brighter,
Than the day before.
I will never love you less,
I will only love you more.

# My Lunar Light

When you were born,
The world was in disarray.
But like your sister,
You brighten the day.

You've grown so quick,
I can hardly keep track.
Picking you up,
Despite my back.

If your sister is my sun,
You are my moon.
One reflecting the other, but
You'll come into your own soon.

I'd like to think,
That I am more able
To raise you better,
To be more mentally stable.

But though I have learned,
A new trick or two.
You continue to surprise me
With everything you do.

You are goofy and giggly,
With an inquisitive mind.
And most important of all,
You are caring and kind.

I know you want to be,
Like your sister, you say.
But remember that you,
Are special in your own way.

Every day you glow brighter,
Guiding us the whole night through.
No matter where you go or who you become,
Remember that I will always love you.

# A Weight

There is a Weight,
Somewhere behind my eye.
It cannot be lifted,
No matter what I try.

I have tried,
Not being sad
And thinking happy thoughts,
But it hasn't helped a tad.

This Weight crushes me,
In a most unpleasant way.
Not gentle pressure,
But more like a boulder may.

The Weight is always there,
No matter what I do.
Trying to run does not help,
When the burden can pursue.

The worst part of it,
At least so I find,
Is the voice the Weight has
And its control over my mind.

What does it say?
I try not to hear.
But the message repeats itself
About what I most fear.

The Weight of expectations
Of who I should have been.
Is the first place the weight
Starts to get underneath my skin.

The Weight of the world,
I fall beneath responsibility
I consider myself guilty
Though none ever accused me.

I let the Weight speak
More than it should.
I demand its silence,
But I have been misunderstood.
The Weight of existence,
Is trying to silence me.
I have fought so long,
Is now where I cease to be?

The only thing left to say,
To this crushing Weight,
Is I will not go yet,
Your failure is clear as I state,

"No, you cannot have me.
I refuse to be taken, so you must wait."

# Enough

Why was I
Never what you'd want
When I had
Everything you'd need?

Not to elevate
myself, or to act superior
But my curiosity hungers,
And your answers would feed.

How was I not enough,
When all I wanted to be
Was what I tried for,
To be a solution for all?

What counts as enough,
Do you even know?
Pushing past my limits,
Rising every time I fall?

I was the rock,
When you needed support.
The calm to handle
Any surprise.

Like Atlas,
I carried upon my shoulders
The weight of my existence
And the burden of your lies.

I don't believe
That you meant to lie
Or that malicious intent
Lay behind every rebuff.

But that breaks me worse,
Knowing the truth.
That somewhere, somehow
I ended up not being enough.

# Wrong

I will never understand
What went wrong.
Where I went wrong
Or why you think
You can do
No wrong.

I sometimes wish
That things could have
Been different.
That you could have
Or we could have,
Been different.

But none of that matters
At least it doesn't now
Not anymore.
There is no love,
Oh how there was, but
Not anymore.

Every conversation hurts
And just feels wrong.
Maybe I overlooked it
This whole time, never right

For each other
Only wrong.

# Hate Me

Hate me if you want,
If you think it's justified.
Call me a cheat and a bastard,
Tell everyone I lied.

I can't expect you to care,
Or try to understand somehow.
Not after years of neglect,
Why would you start now?

Tell yourself whatever will help,
Come to terms with reality.
Problem is, you'll gaslight yourself
And accept a comforting fallacy.

The issue does not lie
In my lack of accepting truth.
But rather, that who I am now,
Is not who I was in my youth.

It may come as a shock,
(and do not misconstrue)
But I'm doing this for me,
This is not about you.

Now, I know it seems unfair,
After always being devoted.
But someone had to love me,
You couldn't- something your actions denoted.

For so long,
I thought myself undeserving of love
That there was more I had to do,
More to prove myself worthy of.

But I was wrong,
Now please let me be.
Let me find myself, and love myself
And you can continue to hate me.

# False Teachings

I didn't need to be taught
How to agree
Or how to listen
Without question.

I didn't need to be taught
Respect for those
That may not even
Deserve it.

I didn't need to be taught
How to sacrifice
Or perform selfless acts
Unconditionally.

I needed to be taught
How to say no.

I needed to be taught
How to respect myself.

I needed to be taught
How to be selfish.

Because now I've been taught
How to be angry
Sometimes toward people
That don't deserve it.

Now I've been taught
How to be bitter
And cynical of anyone new,
Without cause first.

And now I've been taught
That I'm better off alone
Closing my heart to it
Refusing to accept love.

But damn it all,
I have to unlearn,
(Bad habits I've fought.)

Because I choose
To teach my children
What I was never taught.

# The Empath of Least Resistance

So easy, it is,
To be walked on.
Better a hole in the ground,
Than a mountain to climb.

So easy, it is,
To do as you're told.
Better to keep quiet,
Than use your voice.

So easy, it is,
To lose yourself.
Better to lose identity,
Than risk rejection.

So easy, it is,
To play the role they want.
Better to follow instructions,
Than fail on your own.

So easy, it is,
To drown in other's emotions.
Better to suffer those around you,
Than risk feeling your own.

So easy, it is,
To care for others first.
Better to be useful always,
Than left behind.

But the empath
That never meets resistance
Is in for quite a shock,
Because of their greed.

For an empath that overthinks,
Manipulates benevolently to amass affection
Will always end up being alone,
Endeavoring to please all, will not succeed.

# Lost

Call it whatever you want
Passion or light
Fire or fight
But it's missing.
Dripped from my eyes
With every tear
You made me cry.

Nobody understands
What I mean when I say,
"I need to rediscover myself".
Because where did I go?
I'm still here, I never left.
But they don't know,
I've been wandering for years.

When I used to write,
So very long ago,
I used to deliver jokes and puns,
And make people laugh.
Nowadays, it seems
I only make people worry about me
When they read what I create.
Because it's the only time
I am honest with them,
And with myself.

I am trying now though,
To rediscover that spark.
At whatever cost, and doing
Whatever it takes.
I am finding myself slowly,
The old me, but also new parts too.
When the day comes,
And I finish my journey,
I shall walk with my head held high.
For now though, my gaze is low
And I remain lost.

# In Conclusion

I've been struggling
Trying to unravel
The secrets.
Right or wrong
Which one I chose
Not quite sure.
The angel tells me
I'm wrong.
The devil tells me
I'm right.
But which opinion
Is true?
Which do I subscribe to?
I think the answer,
While cliche
Is really very simple.
I need to quit listening,
To anyone, imaginary or not.
I need to start listening to myself,
Whether my gut,
My heart,
Or my head.
All three have valid points,
And one common goal.
Self preservation.

And that is good enough,
For me.

# Dad

I have been known
By many names.
Over the years,
Some nicknames have stuck,
And others have not.
Some names have been
Meant to compliment,
And others have not.
But my favorite title,
A badge I wear with pride,
Is the name of 'Dad'.

My own father,
Was taken from me,
So I had no example to follow.
Which has made it all that harder,
To set one for my own children.
I worry every day,
That today will be the final straw,
And I will do irreparable harm.
The primary goal, is to not be
A primary reason for therapy.

I will keep on
Doing my best.

No matter that it looks
Very different from day to day.
I will keep showing up,
In the big ways and the small.
And maybe someday, somehow
I will be able to prove to my girls
That I love them very much,
And that I deserve to be their
Dad.

# Rest In Peace

I roll my windows down
So my tears can dry
I drive out of town
So I can try
Hiding my screams
And muting my cries
Grieving my dead dreams,
And escaping the lies.

I can't remember
When things changed.
When the light disappeared
Or the passion burned away.
When my love of art,
Or music, or anything
Gave me inspiration
Motivation to live, to stay.

But now I'm numb
And my eyes have clouded.
I stare into the back of my mind
A place deeply shrouded.
I lay me down to sleep,
And hope my soul will keep.
While handfuls of reality
Slowly cover me-

The cenotaph should say
"Rest In Peace
To the person
I used to be."

# One Day

One day,
I will have a body
That you have never
Touched.

One day,
I will have a thought,
That you have never
Influenced.

One day,
I will have a voice,
That you can never
Silence.

One day,
I will have a mind
That you can never
Control.

One day,
I will make choices
That I will never
Doubt.

One day,
I will set boundaries
That will not be
Crossed.

One day,
I will have hope
That you can never
Crush.

One day,
I will have a life
In which you will never
Exist.

One day,
I will be at peace.
I will not punish myself,
For who I am.
I will be kind
I will not call myself a monster
And I will love myself,
One day.